# She
# Persisted

BETHANY HAMILTON

— INSPIRED BY —

# She Persisted

by Chelsea Clinton & Alexandra Boiger

· · · · · · · · · · · · · · · · · · · · · · · · · · · · · · · ·

# BETHANY HAMILTON

· · · · · · · · · · · · · · · · · · · · · · · · · · · · · · · ·

*Written by*
## Maryann Cocca-Leffler

*Interior illustrations by*
## Gillian Flint

**PHILOMEL**

PHILOMEL BOOKS
An imprint of Penguin Random House LLC, New York

First published in the United States of America by Philomel Books,
an imprint of Penguin Random House LLC, 2023

Visit us online at PenguinRandomHouse.com.

Library of Congress Cataloging-in-Publication Data is available.

Printed in the United States of America

HC ISBN 9780593529065
PB ISBN 9780593529072

1st Printing

LSCC

Edited by Talia Benamy and Jill Santopolo.
Design by Ellice M. Lee.
Text set in LTC Kennerley Pro.

*To Ella*

*A fearless girl with big dreams of her own.*

*Persist.*

*Love, Maryann*

Dear Reader,

As Sally Ride and Marian Wright Edelman both powerfully said, "You can't be what you can't see." When Sally said that, she meant that it was hard to dream of being an astronaut, like she was, or a doctor or an athlete or anything at all if you didn't see someone like you who already had lived that dream. She especially was talking about seeing women in jobs that historically were held by men.

I wrote the first *She Persisted* and the books that came after it because I wanted young girls—and children of all genders—to see women who worked hard to live their dreams. And I wanted all of us to see examples of persistence in the face of different challenges to help inspire us in our own lives.

I'm so thrilled now to partner with a sisterhood of writers to bring longer, more in-depth versions of these stories of women's persistence and achievement to readers. I hope you enjoy these chapter books as much as I do and find them inspiring and empowering.

And remember: If anyone ever tells you no, if anyone ever says your voice isn't important or your dreams are too big, remember these women. They persisted and so should you.

Warmly,

*Chelsea Clinton*

# She
# Persisted

..................................................................................

She Persisted: TEMPLE GRANDIN

She Persisted: DEB HAALAND

She Persisted: BETHANY HAMILTON

She Persisted: DOROTHY HEIGHT

She Persisted: FLORENCE GRIFFITH JOYNER

She Persisted: HELEN KELLER

She Persisted: CORETTA SCOTT KING

She Persisted: CLARA LEMLICH

She Persisted: RACHEL LEVINE

She Persisted: MAYA LIN

She Persisted: WANGARI MAATHAI

She Persisted: WILMA MANKILLER

She Persisted: PATSY MINK

She Persisted: FLORENCE NIGHTINGALE

She Persisted: SALLY RIDE

She Persisted: MARGARET CHASE SMITH

She Persisted: SONIA SOTOMAYOR

She Persisted: MARIA TALLCHIEF

She Persisted: DIANA TAURASI

She Persisted: HARRIET TUBMAN

She Persisted: OPRAH WINFREY

She Persisted: MALALA YOUSAFZAI

BETHANY
HAMILTON

# TABLE OF CONTENTS

........................................................

............................

# CHAPTER 1

# *Born to Surf*

Bethany Hamilton was a young champion surfer who tackled any wave that came her way. With focus and grit, she worked hard and succeeded. But when she was thirteen, she faced the biggest challenge of her life, bigger than any wave: she was attacked by a fourteen-foot tiger shark. It was then that she discovered that the skills she perfected in surfing—calm determination, courage, faith, and persistence—would help her overcome any obstacle in life.

. . .

It has been said that Bethany was born with salt water in her veins. Her natural talent for surfing was a gift passed down from her parents.

Before her parents were her parents, they were young teenagers with a passion for surfing, living on opposite sides of the country. Tom Hamilton grew up in Ocean City, New Jersey. The cold East Coast waters, long winters, and a bulky wet suit didn't stop him from riding the waves all year long. Meanwhile, Cheri Lynch, an athletic, daredevil surfer, was living near San Diego in sunny Southern California. She spent her days catching waves up and down the West Coast.

At about the same time, Tom and Cheri both learned that the Hawaiian island of Kauai and its huge waves were drawing top surfers from around the world. Though they had not met each other yet, they both had the same dream—to get there! So, in the early 1970s, with not much more than their backpacks and surfboards, these two young thrill seekers went off to Kauai.

As fate would have it, they ended up hanging out with the same surfer crowd, camping by night and surfing by day. Not only did they find the carefree life and challenging waves they were looking for, they found each other.

It wasn't long before they married and started a family. After having two sons, Noah and Timothy, they welcomed their daughter, Bethany, into the world on February 8, 1990.

The Hamilton family was close-knit and loving. They lived in a small home on the North Shore of Kauai. Sometimes money was tight. Tom worked as a waiter and Cheri cleaned rental condos. Though they were not rich in things, like fancy cars or a big house, they were rich in their

Christian faith, which was the center of their lives. Together they bowed their heads in prayer each day, holding hands around the table.

Growing up on the island of Kauai meant being surrounded by ocean views, the sweet scent of tropical flowers, and chickens! Wild chickens were everywhere! They even nested along the beaches.

As a young girl, Bethany loved doing lots of things, like eating papayas, collecting seashells, and playing with her dog, a shar-pei named Ginger. But her most favorite thing of all was spending her day on the beach and swimming in the clear ocean waters. Her mother jokingly called her a little mermaid because she seemed to spend more time in the sea than on the land.

Though tropical showers sometimes lasted

for days, most of the time Kauai was sunny and warm, perfect for year-round outside activities. Bethany was a rough-and-tumble kid, never worrying about a bruise or a skinned knee. She loved to tag along with her big brothers. She did whatever they did, including roller hockey, surfing, soccer, and skateboarding. Keeping up and competing with her brothers made Bethany fast and fierce. She could do anything her brothers could do, and often better! She was never one to shy away from a challenge. It was clear to her parents and her brothers that Bethany was a fearless, determined, natural athlete.

Since Tom and Cheri were talented surfers, they taught all their children to surf at a young age. It quickly became the family's favorite activity. Every chance they got, they'd toss a cooler and towels into their sandy, beat-up van, nicknamed Blue Crush, tie their five waxed surfboards to the roof, and head to the beach. By the time she was five years old, with her brothers cheering her on, Bethany was surfing . . . and she was good at it!

Soon her parents signed Bethany up for local surfing competitions. Most of these early contests were "push and ride" competitions, meaning the parents would push the kids out to the waves, and the young surfers would ride the wave in. By seven years old, Bethany was able to catch the waves without anyone's help. Big waves didn't scare Bethany. With every day and every wave, she got better and better.

At age eight, Bethany traveled off island to Oahu for her very first state surfing contest. The Rell Sunn competition was named after

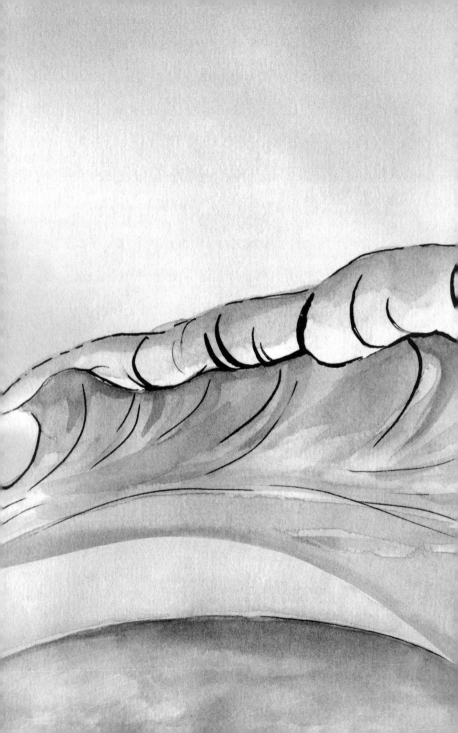

Rell Kapolioka'ehukai Sunn, a female Hawaiian world surfing champion. It was designed for "groms," young surfers like Bethany, who were under the age of thirteen.

Bethany entered two contests for girls aged seven to nine: one for the shortboard and one for the longboard. A shortboard is five to seven feet long, and a longboard is eight to eleven feet long. Bethany's favorite was the shortboard. It was narrow and small and could cut through the water faster than the longboard . . . and Bethany was fast!

Bethany was also smart. Just as her parents had taught her, she took time to read the ocean by watching the patterns of the waves. Throughout the competition Bethany remained calm, confident, and persistent. Every time a powerful wave pulled her under, she'd resurface, climb right back on her surfboard, and bravely face the next big wave. Many times, she used her duck diving skills, grabbing both sides of her board and diving under a wave to set up for the next one.

Bethany surfed well in every heat, when surfers compete in small groups throughout the competition. In the end, when all the scores were tallied, Bethany had won all of her heats. She had even won the division championship!

After cheers and lots of hugs from family, Bethany went home with shiny trophies, two brand new surfboards, and the confidence to keep following her dream to become a profes-sional surfer.

..............................

## *Juggling Life*

B ethany kept winning, but competing was getting expensive. Her family was far from rich, and Bethany was still an amateur, not yet a professional. Amateur surfers don't get any prize money when they win a contest. Entry fees, hotel costs, and travel expenses were adding up.

Her brothers were convinced that Bethany was talented enough to get a sponsor, a company that would pay her to use or wear their surfing products. Her brother Noah became her promoter and contacted major surfing companies, sending videos and photographs of Bethany to get them interested. Rip Curl, a swimsuit company, saw nine-year-old Bethany at a Hawaiian junior surfing event. They were so impressed by Bethany's surfing talent that they signed her. Bethany was thrilled! Now she could help her parents pay for her surfing career *and* wear fun, colorful bathing suits.

Though Bethany loved surfing, church and family were the most important things in her life. The Hamilton family had a deep faith in God and their Christian religion. They belonged to the North Shore Community Church in Kauai, where everyone knew each other, helped each other, and celebrated together.

Her best friend Alana Blanchard and her

family were part of the church too. Bethany and Alana grew up together. They were like sisters—inseparable. They even looked like sisters, with similar golden tans and long blond hair. Together they joined the Kauai Christian Fellowship Church Youth Group, run by a cool pastor, Sarah Hill. Along with hundreds of other middle school kids, they had a blast going to camps, retreats, and rock-and-roll worship events. But more than that, they learned to be kind, help others, and give back to the community.

But juggling church activities, schoolwork, and a surfing career was getting harder and harder. Bethany's calendar was jam-packed. Something had to give. After Bethany completed sixth grade, she and her parents decided that Bethany would be homeschooled. That meant that instead of

going to her local school, Bethany would be taught by Cheri at home. Many of her friends from church and her surfing crowd were being homeschooled too.

Throughout the year, her schoolwork was planned around the surfing conditions. Her mornings began by watching the surfing report on television with her mom. They'd map out the wind, swells, and tides and predict where they would catch the best waves. If conditions were good, they'd grab their surfboards, jump in Blue Crush, and head to the beach, eating breakfast on the way. On those days, the afternoon would be set aside for schoolwork. Though Bethany would have loved to surf all day, she couldn't. Her mom was a tough teacher and made sure Bethany kept up with her studies.

Now thirteen years old, Bethany belonged to the Hanalei girls' surf team. She would often meet up with team members, including Alana, and they'd surf together, giving each other tips and cheering each other on.

They were all training for a big competition: the 2003 National Scholastic Surf Association

(NSSA) Championships, which were to be held in California that spring. Luckily, their North Shore town of Princeville had lots of great surfing spots like Pine Trees, Chicken Wings, Tunnels, and Pauaeaka. Pauaeaka was one of Bethany's favorite places to surf because of its circular, powerful, hollow waves. Waves like those are a surfer's dream! When the top, or crest, of the wave meets the bottom, it forms a hole, sometimes called a tube. Bethany was an expert at "tubing," riding the wave through the tube and exploding out of it like a cannon! Unlike most young surfers, Bethany surfed with her right foot forward and her left foot in the back. In the surfing world it was called being a "goofy-footed" surfer. Goofy or not, this style worked for Bethany.

All the training and practice paid off. In

June 2003, Bethany finished second place in the Open Women's Division of the NSSA Championships, beating women up to twice her age. But that summer, she didn't just sit back and celebrate her success. She surfed almost every day, because she knew that if she wanted to go pro, she had to be at the top of her game.

Sometimes, though, tropical rain showers forced Bethany out of the water. That was the case in late October 2003. After three days of steady rain, Bethany was eager to go surfing. Finally, on October 31, the rain stopped. Even before the sun was up, Bethany and her mom headed to Pauaeaka with their usual on-the-go breakfast. The bright headlights of Blue Crush led the way, driving through deep puddles and low-hanging trees to the beach.

As the sun peeked over the horizon, they could see that the surfing conditions weren't great. Cheri wasn't excited about wasting her morning on so-so waves, but Bethany was itching to surf. She suggested that they check out Tunnels Beach, which was just around the corner from Pauaeaka.

After they parked, Bethany spotted Alana, her dad, Holt, and brother, Byron, pulling up in their black pickup truck. Even though the waves were crummy, Bethany was anxious to get into the water. She convinced her mom to let her stay with Alana and her family. Bethany grabbed her surfboard and headed down to the beach, unaware of what was about to happen.

. . . . . . . . . . . . . . . . . . . . . . . . . . . .

# The Day Life Changed

The sea was practically flat, but after days of rain, Bethany was happy to be in the water.

She hung out near Alana, with Holt and Byron not far away. They all chilled out on their surfboards, looking out to sea, hoping to spot a decent wave. Bethany was enjoying the sun, lying on her blue-and-red surfboard, letting her left arm daggle in the clear water.

Then, from the side of her eye, she noticed a

gray blurry shadow on her left. It got closer and closer. Suddenly she felt a jolt of pressure, a shake, then a quick tug. Almost immediately the water started to turn red. Blood! Her blood! It took her a second to realize what just happened. Her left arm was gone, along with a huge chunk bitten from her surfboard!

Somehow, Bethany didn't panic. In a calm voice, she called to Alana, "I just got attacked by a shark." Bethany was so calm, in fact, that at first Alana thought she was joking. That is, until she saw the blood too. Bethany started paddling toward the shore with one arm. She wasn't feeling any pain. She didn't know it then, but her body was in survival mode—the pain would come later. All she could think of was *Get to the beach . . . Get to the beach.*

When Holt and Byron realized what had happened, they jumped into action. In a flash, Byron sped back to shore to call 911, and Holt raced over to Bethany's side. He took off his shirt and tightly tied it around the stump of Bethany's arm to try to stop the bleeding. Fear hung over them like a black cloud. The shore was a quarter mile away. Could they make it? Were there more sharks? They had to remain focused and get to the beach quick! There was no time to panic.

Holt told Bethany to hang on to his swim shorts as he paddled them both toward shore. Alana was right beside them. Bethany saw the fear in Alana's face and the tears in her eyes. Holt talked to Bethany the whole way to comfort her and keep her awake. Bethany answered his questions, but mostly she prayed, "Please, God. Help me."

It took fifteen minutes to get to the shore, but to Bethany it felt like hours. People were on the beach, ready to help. A nearby surfer took the surf leash off his board and tied it more tightly around Bethany's arm than Holt's shirt had been tied, hoping to stop the bleeding even more. Other beachgoers wrapped Bethany in beach towels to keep her warm. By then, Bethany had lost a lot of blood. Her mind was hazy, and her thoughts wandered. She called out for her mom, wondering if she would ever surf again. Mostly, though, she prayed that she would live.

The ambulance was delayed, and Bethany's situation was quickly getting worse. With the nearest hospital thirty-five miles away, Holt decided that they couldn't wait any longer. He lifted Bethany onto his surfboard and loaded her into the back of his truck. Everyone knew that Bethany needed to get to the hospital, *fast*. Her life depended on it.

The next thing Bethany remembered was waking up in the ambulance, which had met up with Holt's truck. Bethany blinked her eyes open and exhaled. She was very frightened but

relieved. She was finally in the hands of people who would help her. They sped to the hospital, sirens blaring, where a team of doctors and her family were waiting.

The ambulance pulled into the ER, and like a fast-moving wave, frantic nurses and doctors rushed Bethany down the bright white hall. They gave her IV fluids through a tube in her right arm, which was now her only arm. Then came lots of tests and X-rays. Bethany was dazed and shaken but tried to remain calm. Deep down, she knew God would keep her safe.

As the team prepared her for surgery to repair what was left of her arm, her mom and brother Noah rushed in. Just seeing them gave Bethany a huge sense of relief. In a wild coincidence, Bethany's dad was in the hospital, ready to undergo knee surgery in the very same operating room where Bethany was heading! The doctors pushed back his surgery, telling him that the room was needed for a girl who was attacked by a shark. When he found out that it was Bethany, he was crushed. He prayed to God not to take his baby girl.

Bethany was wheeled into the operation room. "You've lost your arm, Bethany," Dr. Rovinsky said gently, "now the focus is on saving your life." Word had spread throughout her church community, and a prayer chain was started across Kauai, surrounding Bethany with love. Questions spun around her head as she drifted off to sleep: How would she paddle out to the waves with one arm? Would she ever surf again? At this point, there was no way to know.

......................................

# CHAPTER 4

# Body and Soul Recovery

After the surgery, Bethany was wheeled into a hospital room where she would spend the next six days healing. She was tired and groggy and slept for most of the first day. With machines beeping and IV tubes attached to her right arm, Bethany looked at the bandaged tender stump of her left arm and realized that her life would never be the same. She began to feel phantom pain in her left arm, pain that her brain was making her think was real, even though the arm wasn't there.

As the fog wore off, she saw that she was surrounded by her family. Tom and Cheri stayed at a nearby hotel so they could be by her side the entire time. They even took turns sleeping in her room. When close friends and family visited, Bethany tried to put on a brave face, but quietly she was trying to make sense of it all. She thanked God for saving her. She was alive. She was grateful for that. But she still had a lot of questions. Why had this happened to her? These were dark moments, but Bethany found peace in her faith. Deep down she knew that God had a plan for her. But what could it be?

While Bethany was recovering in the hospital, her community was busy organizing a big

fundraiser and auction. The Hamilton family would need help with the mounting hospital bills. Word got out! Bethany's shark attack became national news. Donations and cards began pouring in, not only from her community, but from around the world.

News and TV reporters were eager to interview Bethany and her family. But Bethany didn't like the attention or being seen as a victim. While her father handled the growing media frenzy circling outside, Bethany was focused on getting stronger and learning to live without her arm.

By the third day, Bethany was up and about. She worked with physical therapists, who helped her build her muscles in her upper body, right arm, and legs, and occupational therapists, who gave her tips on how to do things with one hand.

Other people were there to help her work through her emotions and give her hope. One of those people was the hospital psychologist. Bethany watched him enter her room, feeling his way until he found a seat at her bedside. The doctor was blind. He asked her a lot of questions about her feelings and her future. But Bethany had a lot of questions for him. Had he always been blind? Was there a cure?

She found out that he had not always been blind and that there was an operation to help him see again, but he wasn't planning to get it. Bethany realized that she would never be able to have a real arm again, and didn't understand why he wouldn't want an operation to get his sight back. He explained that he felt he was able to do more good being blind than being able to see. He had accepted who he was now and found his purpose. Bethany thought that maybe she would be able to do good too. Maybe she had a new purpose too.

Bethany's youth pastor, Sarah Hill, also visited her. She huddled the family in prayer and quoted a Bible verse from Jeremiah:

"'For I know the plans I have for you,' declares the Lord, 'Plans to prosper you and not harm you, plans to give you hope and a future.'"

This verse gave Bethany and her family comfort and strength. Bethany realized that she was truly blessed. She had faith that something good would come out of something bad. The shark had *not* taken away her life. The shark would *not* take away her dreams.

Bethany was starting to feel stronger, but

when she looked down at her body, doubts began to wash through her like a rising tide. How could a person with one arm be a professional surfer? At one point, she told her dad that she would be a surf photographer instead. She figured if she couldn't surf, she would still be up close to the action. She worried her surfing days were over and that Rip Curl would not want to continue sponsoring her. Why would they?

Then came a surprise. A representative from Rip Curl visited her in the hospital. He told Bethany how courageous they thought she had been and how proud they were of her. They still wanted to sponsor her surfing career! Arm or no arm, as soon as her stitches came out, she was going surfing!

On the fourth day, Bethany had another

surgery to continue to repair her wound. Later that day, her dad had some news. He told Bethany that fishermen had caught the shark that attacked her. It was a fourteen-foot, fourteen-hundred-pound tiger shark. Of course, Bethany wanted to know how they knew it was *the* shark. Her dad explained that the sixteen-inch-wide bite out of her surfboard matched the shark's jaws perfectly. Bethany shuddered. "Now the beast can't hurt anyone else," she said.

By the end of her six-day hospital stay, Bethany had a clearer perspective. She *would* surf again! She would become stronger. She would find her purpose. Bethany put her faith in God that He would lead her way. She was ready. She would persist.

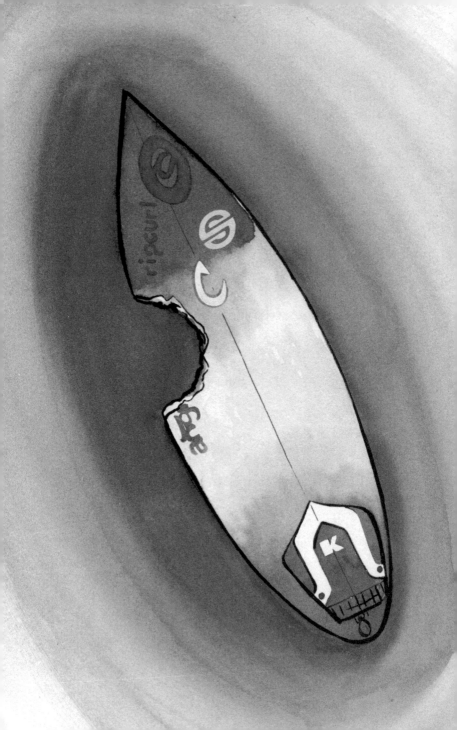

· · · · · · · · · · · · · · · · · · · · · · · · · · ·

## *Surfing Again*

Bethany didn't realize how much she needed two hands until she only had one. Now at home, Bethany tried to do simple things, like cut a sandwich, tie the top of her bathing suit, and put her hair in a ponytail. Everything seemed nearly impossible. And on top of that, because she couldn't get her stitches wet, she was not allowed to go swimming for a whole month. To Bethany, this would be the longest month ever.

One day, as she helped her family prepare lunch, her frustration grew. Even opening a bottle of juice was hard. The family bowed their heads in prayer. They had a lot to be thankful for. As they reached to hold hands around the table, it hit Bethany—she had no hand to offer. The circle was broken—she was broken. But then her brother lovingly placed his hand on her shoulder. The circle was once again complete, just in a new way.

That was it! Bethany would focus on what she could do, instead of what she could not do. She would find new ways of doing things. She patted her stump, which she affectionally called "stumpy." She had faith and grit, and as always, she loved a challenge.

Bethany spent several weeks building her

physical strength and learning to do simple tasks with only one hand. She also had to learn to cope with people staring at her. She got a prosthetic arm, but being strapped to a fake arm felt unnatural and awkward to her, like it was holding her back. Wearing it would have made people more comfortable, but it wasn't comfortable for Bethany. She decided she wasn't going to hide her stump, but instead accept who she was—a girl with one arm!

At the same time, her quiet life had suddenly changed. At thirteen years old, Bethany had become a celebrity. Fan mail piled up and news cameras were everywhere. Magazine and newspaper reporters from around the world requested interviews. National TV news shows wanted to feature her story.

Bethany still didn't like the attention. But after reading some heartfelt letters from other kids who were struggling with lost limbs, Bethany realized that perhaps this was God's plan. Maybe she could inspire others to keep living, keep dreaming, keep working toward their goals, even when times were tough.

The day before Thanksgiving, just one month after the attack, Bethany was finally ready to get back in the water and try surfing again. Though she usually surfed on a shortboard, she chose a longboard for her first ride. She had to adapt, and longboards were wider and would help her balance. As it turned out, it was sort of lucky that Bethany was a goofy-footed surfer. It meant that her right arm could point the way and help her surf! Now she just hoped she could balance herself without her left arm. She would soon find out.

Her family piled in Blue Crush and headed to an out-of-the-way beach where the press wouldn't find her. With a few friends there for moral support, Bethany attached her surfboard leash to her left foot and slowly walked into the clear turquoise water. Suddenly a wave of fear hit her. The last time she was in the ocean had been the day of the shark attack. Would there be another shark out there? Could she do this? Could she surf?

Bethany faced her fears and plunged in. The water enveloped her into a giant embrace. She was home. Now on her stomach, stretched out on her surfboard, she paddled with one arm toward the waves and used her strong legs to propel her. She tried to ride a small wave, but bringing herself to a standing position with only one arm was much harder than she had thought it would be.

Bethany wiped out several times that day, but she persisted. She was NOT giving up. The NSSA Championships were only six months away, and she was going to be there. She kept trying and trying, and finally, with her family and friends cheering her on, she got to her feet, right foot forward, caught a wave, and rode it in. Yes! She could surf!

Over the next few weeks, Bethany kept practicing, pushing herself to master this new way of surfing. With each passing day, she got better and better. Now it was time to get back on her shortboard and tackle the bigger waves, the waves she'd need to surf in professional competitions! But she was frustrated. She needed two hands to hold on to her board, and she didn't have two hands! How would she duck dive under the waves she didn't want to surf? How would she get through the impact zone, the area in the water where the waves break?

Her dad had an idea. He attached a handle to the middle of the top of her surfboard, which would help her get a better grip on the board with just one hand. It worked! She could now hold the surfboard with one hand to duck dive! Bethany trained and trained until she was able to surf even the biggest waves. Now, strong and confident, Bethany was back and ready to compete again.

On January 10, 2004, just ten weeks after losing her left arm in the shark attack, Bethany placed fifth in her age group in the Open Women's

Division of a National Scholastic Surfing Association (NSSA) in Hawaii. Bethany was offered extra time, but she refused. She wanted to be treated like everyone else, and to prove that she wasn't merely surfing, she was competing.

Then, just eight months after the shark

attack, fourteen-year-old Bethany was in California to compete for the 2004 NSSA Championships. The whole world was watching. Bethany made the national finals and took fifth place. "With her ability, will, and heart, she can go far," said her surf coach, Ben Aipa. And she did. That same year, Bethany received the Teen Choice Awards Courage Award in front of a cheering crowd.

The following year, Bethany went even further—she took first place at the 2005 NSSA Championships! With her competitive spirit, talent, and determination, Bethany proved to herself and the world that she could, once again, compete at an expert level. There was no holding her back.

CHAPTER 6

· · · · · · · · · · · · · · · · · · · · · · · · · · ·

## *Still Inspiring*

After the attack, Bethany's surfing career and popularly began to soar. And at the same time, her Christian faith and unstoppable spirit helped inspire others.

Bethany realized that God's plan for her was to tell the world her story—a story about how one shark tried to snatch away a dream and how one young girl fought back with grit and faith. Her story spread, and so did her message.

In 2005, Bethany went to Thailand on a mission trip with a Christian relief organization. The year before, a massive wave, called a tsunami, had devastated Thailand's coastal communities, washing away homes, fishing villages, and lives. Understandably, families and their children were afraid to get back into the ocean. When Bethany lost her arm, she had been afraid too, and now she wanted to help others face their fear. On a beach in Thailand, Bethany set up a surfing camp. Little by little, she coaxed kids to once again enjoy the water.

The media also continued to share Bethany's story. Magazines like *Sports Illustrated* and *Life* featured her. She appeared on news shows like *20/20* and *Inside Edition* and was even interviewed by Oprah. In 2004, she wrote her

bestselling autobiography, *Soul Surfer*, which inspired the 2011 movie of the same name. Actress AnnaSophia Robb played Bethany in the movie, but Bethany performed all the surf stunts herself. In addition to the movie, there were several documentaries made about her life. In 2014, Bethany was voted Favorite Comeback Athlete at the Nickelodeon Kids' Choice Awards.

In 2007, at the age of seventeen, Bethany realized her dream of becoming a professional surfer.

She went on to be ranked as one of the top twenty female professional surfers in the world, traveling all over the globe to compete in places like Australia, Portugal, Brazil, Fiji, and more.

Through it all, Bethany never accepted any favors to make her road easier. She wanted to compete fairly, and she did. But there was one thing that wasn't fair: the prize money for female surfers was about half of what the men received! Women surfers pushed for equal pay. After all, many of them—including Bethany—could out-surf the men. Finally, in September 2018, the World Surfing League announced that male and female winners would receive the same prize money.

On Aug 4, 2017, at the age of twenty-seven, Bethany was inducted into the Surfers Hall of Fame in Huntington Beach, California. After the ceremony, the new Hall of Fame surfers traditionally put their hands in wet cement to leave behind handprints. Bethany put both feet and her one hand into the cement and added the message: *Always Hope—Love, Bethany.*

Bethany married youth minister Adam Dirks

in 2013, and now they have a surfing family of their own. They live in Hawaii with their three sons.

In addition to being a mother and professional surfer, Bethany is a mentor and public speaker.

She continues to merge her unstoppable attitude with her Christian faith, and she teaches classes that help people follow their dreams, handle problems, become physically stronger, and deepen their faith. Along with her family and friends, she created the Beautifully Flawed Foundation, which offers retreats and conferences to empower, unite, and inspire people with limb differences.

To this day, Bethany continues to give people hope and encourages them to never give up on their dreams. Throughout her life, Bethany persisted.

You can too.

# HOW YOU CAN PERSIST

*by Maryann Cocca-Leffler*

Bethany had big dreams and goals and found ways to make a difference. You can too! Here are a few things you can do:

1. Try doing something new! Even if it's scary, challenge yourself and face your fears!

2. Invite, include, and support people with all types of abilities. Find ways to make events and activities accessible so everyone can join in.

3. If you're faced with a challenge or big life change, think of it as an adventure. Find ways to adapt and never give up!

4. Make someone's life better by volunteering in your community, whether through a church or another place where people gather.

5. Find a new way of doing something.

6. Learn about oceans and sea life. Visit a beach or a local aquarium.

7. Keep our oceans and waterways clean by picking up plastic bottles and trash.

8. Learn to swim.

9. Learn first aid.

10. Persist. Never give up on your dreams.

# ACKNOWLEDGMENTS

......................................

Sincere gratitude to Chelsea Clinton for creating the She Persisted biography series and for inviting me to be part of the Persisterhood.

Thank you to my editors, Talia Benamy and Jill Santopolo, for your guidance and belief in me as an author, and to your team of hardworking copy editors and fact-checkers.

To Bethany Hamilton, whose story of strength and courage inspires others to focus on what they can do, not what they cannot do, and to live their best lives.

# ☙ References ❧

**BOOKS:**
..................

Anderson, Karen, and Lehia Apana. *Essential Hawaii*. Fodor's Travel. 2021.

Hamilton, Bethany. *Soul Surfer*. New York: Pocket Books, 2004.

Kempton, Jim. *Women on Waves: A Cultural History of Surfing*. New York: Pegasus Books, 2021.

Nelson, Chris, and Demi Taylor. *Surfing: Skills, Training, Techniques*. Marlborough: Crowood Press, 2017.

Walsh, Jenni L. *She Dared: Bethany Hamilton.*

New York: Scholastic, 2019.

## FILMS:

*Soul Surfer.* Tristar Pictures, 2011

*Bethany Hamilton: Unstoppable.* Documentary.

Lieber Films, 2019.

## WEBSITES:

BethanyHamilton.com

BeautifullyFlawedFoundation.com

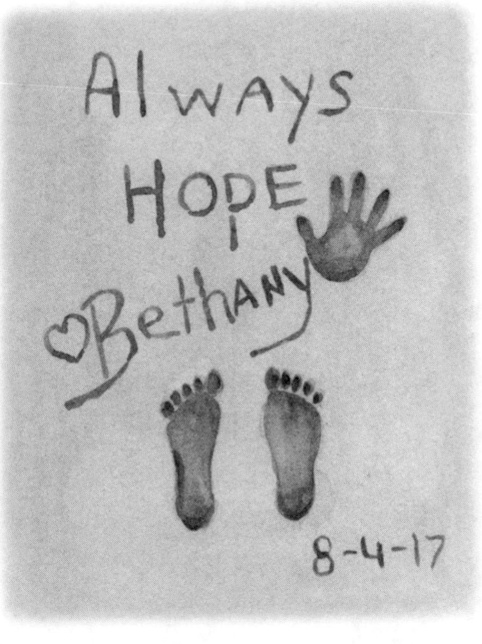
Always
HOPE
Bethany
8-4-17

MARYANN COCCA-LEFFLER is an award-winning author and illustrator of over seventy books for children. Her recent picture books include the NCTE Orbis Pictus honor book *Fighting for YES! The Story of Disability Rights Activist Judith Heumann*, illustrated by Vivien Mildenberger, and *We Want to Go to School! The Fight for Disability Rights*, coauthored with her daughter, Janine Leffler. Both books were awarded Gold Standard Selections by the Junior Library Guild. Maryann's family and New England roots have inspired many books along the way, including *Clams All Year*, *Bus Route to Boston*, and the picture book *Janine*. Her other recent books include *The Power of YET* and her debut middle grade novel, *Heart Stones*, a mystery set on the coast of Maine, where Maryann happily resides.

Photo credit: *Kristin Leffler*

You can visit Maryann Cocca-Leffler online at
MaryannCoccaLeffler.com
or follow her on Twitter
@MCLeffler
and on Instagram
@MaryannCoccaLeffler

GILLIAN FLINT has worked as a professional illustrator since earning an animation and illustration degree in 2003. Her work has since been published in the UK, USA and Australia. In her spare time, Gillian enjoys reading, spending time with her family and puttering about in the garden on sunny days. She lives in the northwest of England.

You can visit Gillian Flint online at
gillianflint.com
or follow her on Twitter
@GillianFlint
and on Instagram
@gillianflint_illustration

CHELSEA CLINTON is the author of the #1 *New York Times* bestseller *She Persisted: 13 American Women Who Changed the World*; *She Persisted Around the World: 13 Women Who Changed History*; *She Persisted in Sports: American Olympians Who Changed the Game*; *Don't Let Them Disappear: 12 Endangered Species Across the Globe*; *It's Your World: Get Informed, Get Inspired & Get Going!*; *Start Now!: You Can Make a Difference*; with Hillary Clinton, *Grandma's Gardens* and *Gutsy Women*; and, with Devi Sridhar, *Governing Global Health: Who Runs the World and Why?* She is also the Vice Chair of the Clinton Foundation, where she works on many initiatives, including those that help empower the next generation of leaders. She lives in New York City with her husband, Marc, their children and their dog, Soren.

You can follow Chelsea Clinton on Twitter
@ChelseaClinton
or on Facebook at
facebook.com/chelseaclinton

ALEXANDRA BOIGER has illustrated nearly twenty picture books, including the She Persisted books by Chelsea Clinton; the popular Tallulah series by Marilyn Singer; and the Max and Marla books, which she also wrote. Originally from Munich, Germany, she now lives outside of San Francisco, California, with her husband, Andrea, daughter, Vanessa, and two cats, Luiso and Winter.

Photo credit: *Vanessa Blasich*

You can visit Alexandra Boiger online at
alexandraboiger.com
or follow her on Instagram
@alexandra_boiger

# Read about more inspiring women in the

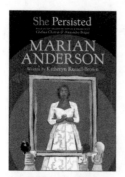

## She Persisted
BASED ON THE BESTSELLING PICTURE BOOK BY
Chelsea Clinton & Alexandra Boiger
### MARIAN ANDERSON
Written by Katheryn Russell-Brown

## She Persisted
BASED ON THE BESTSELLING PICTURE BOOK BY
Chelsea Clinton & Alexandra Boiger
### VIRGINIA APGAR
Written by Dr. Sayantani DasGupta

## She Persisted
BASED ON THE BESTSELLING PICTURE BOOK BY
Chelsea Clinton & Alexandra Boiger
### PURA BELPRÉ
Written by Meg Medina with Marilisa Jiménez García

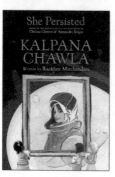

## She Persisted
BASED ON THE BESTSELLING PICTURE BOOK BY
Chelsea Clinton & Alexandra Boiger
### KALPANA CHAWLA
Written by Raakhee Mirchandani

## She Persisted
BASED ON THE BESTSELLING PICTURE BOOK BY
Chelsea Clinton & Alexandra Boiger
### CLAUDETTE COLVIN
Written by Lesa Cline-Ransome

## She Persisted
BASED ON THE BESTSELLING PICTURE BOOK BY
Chelsea Clinton & Alexandra Boiger
### ELLA FITZGERALD
Written by Andrea Davis Pinkney

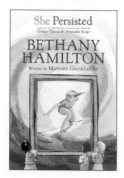

## She Persisted
BASED ON THE BESTSELLING PICTURE BOOK BY
Chelsea Clinton & Alexandra Boiger
### BETHANY HAMILTON
Written by Maryann Cocca-Leffler

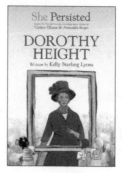

## She Persisted
BASED ON THE BESTSELLING PICTURE BOOK BY
Chelsea Clinton & Alexandra Boiger
### DOROTHY HEIGHT
Written by Kelly Starling Lyons

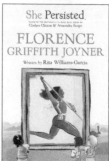

## She Persisted
BASED ON THE BESTSELLING PICTURE BOOK BY
Chelsea Clinton & Alexandra Boiger
### FLORENCE GRIFFITH JOYNER
Written by Rita Williams-Garcia

# She Persisted series!

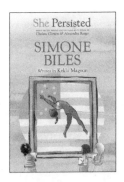

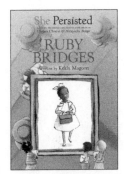

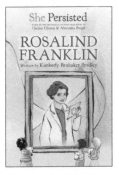

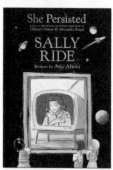

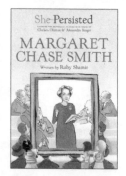

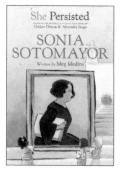

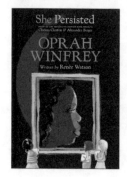

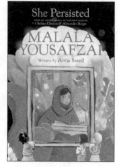

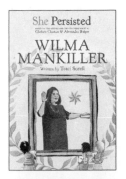

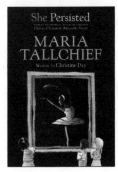

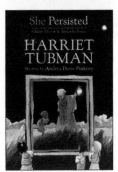